Nandita Nandan, began her journey with words at the tender age of 12, amidst the timeless charm of Varanasi, a city where the Ganges flows like a hymn, and every corner breathes inspiration. One August day, as the warm winds of the season stirred the air, she sat by her window, watching the world shift under the monsoon sky. In that moment, without any intention other than a spark of curiosity, she wrote her first poem about the rain. What started as a simple, playful act soon grew into a deep connection with words, eventually leading her to create a book, carrying the essence of her soul and the spirit of the city she calls home.

INVISIBLE STRING

NANDITA NANDAN

PROLOGUE

In your hands lies a collection of poetries
This book is a tribute to someone (the author)
whose words will show you the beauty of writing.
I won't say these will be the best poetries you've read, but
surely an incomparable one.
They are delicate offerings from the poet
Each word is a sigh, each verse a heartbeat-crafted in
silence, dedicated to one and filled with raw, unspoken
power of love.
Yet like the finest treasure, they are
They carried the weight of the devotion too deep to fade,
and deserve to be held, to be shared.
This collection is not just poetry-it is the act of preserving
something fragile yet boldly written Something deep
personal yet universality felt. Like the secret letters never
meant to be sent, these verses held their place in the
note pad kept safe in the heart of the poet.
But now this book exists, a quiet unveiling of
serenity now brought in light.
As you journey through these pages,
you will find how words
are not just a means of expression
but a sanctuary for devotion.

A Note to the readers

I am not the author, nor the publisher,
but rather someone who deeply admires
her talent and wanted to ensure
her art finds its way into your hands.
This book is a tribute to her talent, and my small
contribution has been to bring her artistry to you.
These poems are not confined to a particular genre
or theme; they are an expression of raw,
unfiltered feelings, woven together
from the fabric of life itself.
This book is a celebration of emotions
in all their complexity, understanding,
empathy,and reminding us that it's okay to feel deeply,
to embrace the beauty of being human.

Thank you for allowing these verses
to become a part of your story.

May they speak to your heart
and leave an impression on your soul.

To the Author:

You asked me what will be the first thing
I'll tell you if you've lost your memory
I said "your name of course"
But yes I was wrong,
you deserve to be called a "poet" first.

This book is yours
Every page captures your essence
Every word conveys it's beauty of being written
It's not just a book but a tribute
to your extraordinary talent

-Someone who may not promise you
the stars, but will always be there to
heal all your scars

There's something magical about firsts—
their innocence, their honesty,
and the stories they tell.
As you turn this page, you hold in your hands
poet's very first attempt at capturing emotions,
dreams, and fleeting thoughts in the form of poetry.
It carries a unique charm—raw passion,
and the courage to put thoughts into words.
As the poet's debut work, it holds a special place,
not just for the one who wrote it, but for all
who have the privilege to read it.

May it remind you of the beauty
that lies in beginnings.

12 AUG. 2021

IS IT?

Is it rain or heaven, or the sky of
colours that sparkles
like blossoming flower bud that
accompany the tears of one's eye.
Is it rain or the treasure
that is washed off
with bitter sweet memories
of dusty shelter.

Nandita Nandan

From the depths of the ocean
a field of lavender blooms
a symbol of hope
amidst the chaos
that surrounds it
In this collection of poetry
we explore the beauty and
mystery of this unlikely phenomenon
drawing parallels
between the fragility of life
and the enduring power of the human spirit
But as we journey through these pages
we are reminded that beauty
can emerge from pain, struggle,
fear, and chaos.
Through the lens of this captivating image
we delve into themes of growth, change
and the unyielding force of nature
to inspire and heal the soul
while challenging our perceptions
of what it truly means to find hope
in the midst of adversity.

Your eyes

I am too shy to look into your eyes
As i am afraid
that you might catch all my lies
hidden deep inside
my every good bye

Nandita Nandan

Zoning out, piled up stack
messed up desk, out of track
and in my head, anxiety is back
coping up with frustration
coffee sip with lack of concentration
thoughts to have it perfect
with silly calculation
suffocation due to self accusations
bunch of therapist session but still
the lack of application
making it worse being pessimist
the idea of being perfectionist
is the only thing i could think of to be honest
the stress of being on top as promised
pending wish list is the indication
I don't want anymore vindication
the only dedication left within me
is too reach my destination.

Invisible strings

I was never meant to recieve
the hand full of flowers
neither i deserved love
of those late night hours
either be those cringy text
copy pasted of browser
i was never supposed to have
that love at first sight encounter
we were better off as stranger
as you were already her perfect partner
stupid of me to think the moment was ours
the third of december was written for her
the sweater that smelt like home
was actually hers
the love letter with ink smeared treasure
was actually written for body pleasure
nothing like i thought
it was just another love affair
happened in leisure.

Nandita Nandan

If only you could my visit my head
explore those am i enough poster
bumping into the dustbin of words
left unsaid
hit by those self doubt winds
at most turning you colder
Will you rate all the portrait
painted of those monsters
remember to plant some seeds there
even though i have enough of them
to make me bleed
make sure to paint something
I won't mind even it's another scar
as to me it's stunning
hope those unheard melodies
makes you dance
being played on the broken strings of guitar
wish this time you won't ignore the hints
that how deeper your words
have left imprint
don't forget to walk down the crossover
to find my leftover
only if you looked closer
whenever i said "I am to fine to be a loner"
I know this trip will be one hell of roller coaster
but it will be entertaining to find me dead
will you mind if i rest myself on your shoulder
for the last time
before my body gets more colder.

Invisible strings

She thinks the world don't need her
as she don't have the right to be her
whenever she tries to change for better
the society types
another judgmental letter
those looks with gossiping mouth
have made her heart doubt
the raised eyebrow
adorning the smug face
the taunt in disguise
has filled her empty space
the attempt
to be like those ideal disney princess
have already killed
the rising empress
to fit the cindrella shoes perfectly
she lost the diamond crown deliberately
she was someone
who could rise from ashes
only if she was given a chance
to born again from scratches
she wasn't supposed to hate her bruises
they were not something useless

they were the sign that
she won those battles
breaking all those
toxic worldly shackles
in the end
she couldn't be just some fallen angel
not even just a fighter

**she was someone with pen
and identity of writer..**

Invisible strings

How could a heart like yours
is willing to love a heart like mine
as soul like yours
only cures
the way you love
is definitely an art
your light brown eyes
can perfectly lure
to hard to predict
if its a end
or a new start.

Nandita Nandan

Emptiness within me
is the heaviest burden
tears swept from my eyes
have witnessed many goodbyes
My lips curled in dimple
is nothing but artificial
my slow and steady giggles
is expert in hidding many scribbles
cracked numerous jokes
but none noticed the pain disguised
laughed with many
but found none when life was messy
Many hugged me
but none found the reason
behind my eyes crying blood.

Invisible strings

Wish it was easier
to forget those days spent together
with each lit up cigarette
i feel nothing but pleasure
it's getting hard to breathe
with all these scars
hidden beneath your sweater
i don't know if it's the change
in fate or weather
despite me being heather
we are not perfectly together
autumn has came
with each falling leaf
I am trying to forget your name
dust have covered our photo frame
sophisticated blunder
that I can't even complain
even we won't be able to dance
with eachother this rain.

It's easy for you right
being dead is far better
than watching your love
turn into red
you broke your promise about us
being forever
now it's just me
trying to move on for better.

Invisible strings

Let's get lost
untill it's fall in september
somewhere far away
where the valley is named forever
play the soundtrack till twenty nine
with all the flashback
in repeat on last night
where will we go after it's over
will we return half weight like soldiers
or maybe we will drink
untill we have strong hangover
but what if this time we don't leave
let's just steal the time being a thief
will you mind to play your antique guitar
untill I ask another wish
on shooting star.

Nandita Nandan

Scar leave me politely
please just for a while
leave me slightly
before making me gasp for air unkindly
instead of whispering
how I look tonight
I will yell the way i survived
the way I tried and how I arrived
believe me I am strong
but who knows maybe I can be wrong
self doubt, negativity
and messed up brain lifelong
these are some
but the list is quite long
It's not tough for scar to make it this far
terrible thoughts having head in knot
busy gazing mirror
despite it being trickster
making me believe, I am the spinster
scars through my eyes
are the reason of my many goodbyes
anxiety holds power
insecurity runs deep permanents scar
no one can counter
i sometimes wonder am I the only one?
then I remember
after all I am none
I am depressed and stressed
but no one knows
cause first i am someone unexpressed.

Invisible strings

The magic she carried
was long gone forgotten
the way her giggles
filled the melody in the kindergarden
was nowhere to be found
either be that laughter sound
or how she used to trip on the ground
nothing felt like her now
as if that her was drowned
the innocence her eyes radiated
has somewhere faded
the cheeks that was fascinated
the blush that adorned it
has eliminated
the smile which illuminated
is now shut feeling frustrated
whatever this poetry illustrated
is how she is devastated
the one who waited for her own birthday
is still stuck in yesterday
hoping to run away
awaiting for her own death someday.

Nandita Nandan

The sun sets low on the horizon
as the moon rises up high
a moment of beauty and surprise
As they share the same sky
the stars begin to twinkle
as the moon
takes the center stage
a moment of magic and wonder
as nature turns the page.

Invisible strings

Sincere kisses mixed with jealousy
a place where you might fall
for your own enemy
some might be happy after seeing tragedies
but will they be elated
with the news of pregnancies
spicy gossips after every new surprise
here lips shiver with truth
while they smirk after lies
here you will find more exceptions
in crush list,than those popular plot twist
race to be a queen bee
by having number of guys
while that one girl
still have him framed in her eyes
you will find more chemistry
between every new hookups
while your textbook lay there
with no check-ups
eachday begins with a breakup
while some search
for new tutorial of makeup

Nandita Nandan

No one knows
how many suffers heartbreak
well you don't even know
when love might flourish
with a mare handshake
you will know this place as the time flies
this place is interesting isn't it
where you might even fall
over sip of coffee
and high school is the name
of this wonderful story.

Invisible strings

In this world of hate, judgement,
power and lust
she is someone
made of magical pixie dust
you can never find her in this world
as she lives far away
among stars and fantasies
it's universe tragedy
that they lost her in different galaxy
she had the brightest smile
to hide her pain
she can even make you feel drunk
without any champagne
she is someone with unknown mysteries
one who can conquer
all the cosmic victories
but who knew
she will become a forgotten history
only if that night
she tried to rose from ashes
before drawing stars on her wrist
like it's canvas.

Your words used to flow
like a gentle stream
a soothing sound
like a peaceful dream
your voice used to warm me
full of grace
a joy to hear, like a sweet embrace
but once I thought my heart was true
and I was sure, I loved only you
but now my feelings have changed
and my heart feels so estranged
I don't know what went wrong
or how my feelings could have gone
but now I see the truth so clear
and I know you no longer dear
It's hard to let go of what we once had
But I know it's time
to move on and be glad
for there's a new path that lies ahead
and I'll find love again
without any dread.

Invisible strings

From shattered dreams
and broken bones
a childhood lost, a life unknown
a heart that's heavy, a mind that's torn
a soul that's weary, a spirit worn
but through the pain, they found their way
to heal the hurt, and find a way
to help the lost, and guide the way
to heal the wounds, of yesterday
and though the scars may never fade
they found a light, a new crusade
to lift the broken, and ease the pain
to help the troubled find their way
for in the darkness, they found their light
a path to heal, and make things right
to lift the broken, and guide the way
to help the lost find hope today
so though the past may haunt their soul
they found a way to make things whole
to heal the hurt, and find a way
to light the path, for a brighter day.

~ someone with broken childhood

Nandita Nandan

But love itself
with a voice so cold
whispers a truth
that must be told
"I have slit throats
far more beautiful than yours"
A reminder that not every time
love cures.

Invisible strings

The sun was shining bright and clear
And I felt happy, with nothing to fear
I walked along the sandy shore
And felt the waves crashing more
and more
But then I saw a strange sight
A mermaid sitting in the light
She beckoned me to come near
And whispered secrets in my ear.
She told me tales of the deep
And showed me treasures I could keep
She promised me a life of ease,
If only I would follow her with ease.
But then I heard a sound so loud,
And I woke up, feeling quite proud
For I had faced my deepest fear,
And found the courage to persevere.

Nandita Nandan

She stand there looking out of window
with her hair falling side ways
the bed tucked neatly with a tear soaked
pillow the locket adorning her neck,
counting days
her lips beautifully painted in red
wildly dressed in violet georgette
but still it holds no meaning
other then being smudged in death
the neon lights are flashing
the music abstract and clear
she must be waiting for her lover
to take her from there
but she is doing what she must do
to make things end
several men come to her
when the moon is high
they pay for her body, uttering sweet lies
she is a woman of street
she is living life on it's edge
with her body as trade
with each new person
she have made her body more degrade
she knows
that she is breaking all the rules
but she is a woman of the night
and this is how she pay her dues

Invisible strings

She dream of a better life
where she don't have to sell her soul
but for now, she is a prostitute
a woman of the late night
and she must keep on walking these streets
until she find the morning light
so if you see her on the corner
with her hair tangled like mess
don't judge her for her choices
or the tears in her eyes
she is the woman of the night
doing what she have to do
and she is just trying to survive like us
and you can see it in her eyes.

Nandita Nandan

In an old, dusty corner of the room
A letter lay, forgotten and consumed.
It's edges were frayed
it's ink faded
But it's words were alive,
and they waited.
Years had passed, and it was lost in time,
But now a little kid had found it, so fine.
He didn't know what it meant
or who it was for,
But he loved to read it,
and he wanted more.
The words were like magic
they took him away,to a time long ago
to a place far away.
He imagined the people,
the places, the things,
And he felt like he was flying on wings.
The letter was old, but it was new to him,
And he read it again,
with a smile so grim.
He wished
he could show it to someone else,

Invisible strings

But he knew it was his,
and he kept it close.
So he read it again,
and read it with pride
And he knew that the letter
would always be by his side.
For it, was a treasure,
a gift from the pashim
And it would always be with him,
until the very last.

Nandita Nandan

I am too shy to look at you
to meet your gaze, to see it through
for in your eyes
I fear I'll find all the pain and hurt
I've left behind
every goodbye, a piece of me
a part of my heart, set free
and though I try to hide it well
the truth is there in every farewell
The words I say, they're just a mask
a way to hide the pain that lasts
but in your eyes, I see the truth
the pain and hurt, the loss of youth
so I'll keep my gaze, downcast and shy
and hope that you won't see the lie in every goodbye
I long for a part of you
who will hold onto me
like those promises you made when we were new
but if you catch a glimpse of what's inside
the pain and hurt, the tears I've cried
know that it's real and it's all true
and that every goodbye, is a part of you
So please be gentle with my heart
for it's been broken, right from the start
and though I may be too shy to see
know that every goodbye, is a part of me

Invisible strings

If my eyes became your lens
would you unravel my sins with your hands?
How deeply must you touch me
to feel the weight of my secrets
reel and real?
would the scars etch upon my skin
tell tales of battles lost and won within?
How much must you see me to understand
the marks left by life's heavy hand?
And if hatred were your guide
how close must you come to me
to find the devil inside?
How much must you kiss me
to know every story behind my battered lips?
How many masks must I shed
before you see the truth that lies beneath?
How many pieces of my shattered heart
must you gather to understand
the mosaic of my existence?
After this
I am again left with another question
on how much question you must answer
to be "the one "?

She was the one
who remembered your favorite food order
she is definitely a charecter
written by some professional author
because on Monday mornings
she'd ask about your weekend days
as you stumbled over words
still waking up from haze
she would you offer her umbrella
and walk in rain herself
like the kindest quote you highlighted
in that book lying on shelf
she was the one who made you feel seen
in a world that often leaves us blind
in world full of red flags
you will find her in green
when your payment in therapy ever gets declined
remember about the girl who fixed you
with her one smile
remembering every detail
no matter how small or grand
she'd pick up your call
even with cooking oil on her hand
she would text you with soapy hands
she will try to fix your every scar
like man in love likes fixing his girl's hair strands
when they kill innocence and prioritises the cruel
she was the one who made kindness look cool
The colors around her seems to come alive
as if they're painting a picture that will survive

Invisible strings

the greens are greener
and the blues are bluer
and the world is cruel
just seems to be a rumour
So let me highlight that kind quote again
"God made sadness and sent her as apology"

Nandita Nandan

From the pages of your book
you came to me
a mystery wrapped in words
a world to see
your characters so real,
your story so true
I fell in love with you
before I even knew
I read your words with bated breath
each sentence a kiss
each chapter a death
I couldn't put your book down
I was hooked
and as I turned the pages, i was cooked
you spoke to me in ways i never known
your words a symphony
your voice a tone
a melody that played inside my head,
a song that filled my soul with dread
for I knew that when your book was done
I'd have to say goodbye
I'd have to run away
from the world you created for me
back to the real world, where I'd be free
but still I fell in love with you
with your words, your story
your point of view

Invisible strings

and though we may never meet in person
I'll always cherish you
my favorite version.

Nandita Nandan

I stay there in the corner so still
and watch the girl
who feels the chill
I see the wonders, I see the pain
of how a teenager stutter
she sees her imperfections
and she sees the rejection
only if she knew
she could be an exception
she sees her flaws
and she sees the pain
she often wonders
if she could start again
she sees her pimple, her fizzy hair
to her it's not even fair
she sees her dress
she sees her crooked teeth
now she prays
to be someone else beneath
in her mind, doubt and fear
are often seen
as she is just another insecure teen.

Invisible strings

I see her strength
and her hidden cause
I see her kindness
and her gentle heart
and I know that she'll find
a brand new start
so I tell her, as she looks at me
that she's beautiful
and she's meant to be
she is stuck in imperfections lies
but she is the beauty
beyond disguise
For though she may not see it now
I know that she'll find her wow
but i see more than just her flaws
for in her eyes
I see her spark
a light that shines
even in the dark
but here's the twist if you please
for I am not what I may seem
I am not a person, flesh and bone

but a mirror
hanging all alone
so though I am just glass and frame
I see the girl who's now
not the same
and as she smiles
and she wipes her tears
I know that she has conquered
all her fears
for she has seen herself
in a brand new way and she's ready
to face a brand new day.

Invisible strings

A house captain,
with a heart full of pride,
Tries her best,
but the teacher's words make her hide.
She works so hard,
but her efforts are in vain,
For the teacher always finds something
to complain.
She wears her best attire,
and feels so proud,
But the teacher points out
her falling hair
that's not allowed to appear
She tries to smile, but it feels so fake
And she's worried
the teacher will notice,
and she'll be a mistake.
But then she remembers
that she's doing her best
And that's all that matters,
above all the rest.
She knows that she's trying,
and that's worth something more,
Than all the teacher's words,
that cut her to the core.

For though she may feel small,
and unsure of herself
She knows that her efforts
are worth more than wealth.
And though the teacher
may point out her flaws
She knows that
she's doing her best, and
that's worth applause.
So let this house captain be
an inspiration to us all
For she's fighting her fears,
and she's standing tall.
And though the teacher
may not see, or understand
She knows that
she's doing her best,
and that's worth a helping hand

Invisible strings

The pillow of an insecure teen
feels the weight
of something left unseen
the pillow feels the weight of doubt
and hears the fears
that don't shout
It's soaked with tears
both day and night
as they struggle
to be their own knight
It cradles them in gentle care
and holds them close
through every scare
It's stained with makeup
smeared and wet
as they cry themselves
to sleep upset
but in that pillow
there's a spark
A light that shines
through the dark

Nandita Nandan

For though, their fears
may seem so strong,
they can rise above them lifelong
And in the end, she'll find her worth
A sign that she belongs
on this earth.
So if you see a pillow stained
With tears and fears, and all that's pained
Know that it's a place of grace
For an insecure teen's embrace.

Invisible strings

Thousands of unsaid words
etched by the typewriter's keys
Speak of my forbidden love
that's hidden with ease.
Memories, like wildfire
that burn and consume
Are a testament to our love
that's hidden in gloom
The calligraphy of our love
is both beautiful and dark
A symbol of our passion,
that left its mark
The cold winter air,
that marks the beginning of Christmas
Belies the agony I feel,
that's hidden in my abyss
The pauses between each line,
are like a heartbeat's rhythm,
A secret code that speaks of
our love's hidden emblem

Nandita Nandan

Each sip of wine,
that you so expertly poured,
Intoxicated me,
with a love that never bored
Forbidden love,
like a sweet and tantalizing fruit
Is more sweeter
when it's hidden from view
So I write these lines
with a heart that's true
And keep your name hidden
like Romeo and Juliet knew.

Invisible strings

As fear grips my heart
you might wear different hues
I dread the thought of losing the "me"
that once knew you
I wish I didn't need sleep to be in your arms
where dreams hold us close, free from alarms
was it my fault that i found peace in your mess?
Or that I can't be her, no matter how hard I impress?
Does it take my absence
a last goodbye
for you to hold me in thoughts, as time slips by?
Now I even try to find you when I am with you
haunted by shadows
of what we've been through
when you're thousands of years late
don't seek my ruins, as fear grips my heart
you might wear different hues
I dread the thought of losing the "me"
that once knew you
I wish I didn't need sleep to be in your arms
where dreams hold us close, free from alarms
was it my fault I found peace in your mess?
Or that I can't be you forever
no matter how hard I impress?
Does it take my absence, a last goodbye
for you to hold me in thoughts, as time slips by?

Nandita Nandan

I try to drown the noise in everything but him
but the silence he leaves
echoes louder than any distraction
from admiring from far to kissing his lips
standing on my toes
he caressed all my scars
even before he got his hands
beneath my plain clothes
In me insecurities runs deep but still
he calls me flawless from bone to skin
but then I don't question it much
as it's just him in me within.

Invisible strings

Length of cloth and time of clock
should never be used to define and mock
a girl's character, her worth,
her grace, and her value is not defined
by the fabric she displays
It's time to break free
from all those old ways
to celebrate women
in all their different displays
to see them for who they truly are
not just a length of cloth
or a time on a clock that's far
a girl's character is not defined
by the clothes she wears
or the time she bides
It's her heart, her soul,
and her spirit within,
that makes her beautiful,
unique, and akin
so let's break free from these old traditions
and celebrate women
in all their different compositions
let's see them for who they truly are
and appreciate their beauty
both near and far.

Nandita Nandan

love entrance is dramatic
it's never simple
and comes with some magic
All those waiting for love should know
It's a queen of drama
ready to show
It's a rollercoaster ride
But don't worry It will arrange you
a partner to hug you tight
But when love finally arrives
It's worth all the drama
and the drives.
love is a journey with ups and downs
it has the power to hand you the crown
but it can also make you
the centre clown
So don't be afraid of
love's grand entrance
It's worth the wait and the suspense
Just buckle up and enjoy the ride
And let love be your utmost guide

Invisible strings

she used to be so wild and free
but now she is just a memory
she used to dance under the moon light
now she is writing
about the darkest night
she used to laugh
until her side did ache
now if she ever laugh
it's always by mistake
her once innocent shining eyes
have now started to hide the cries
but deep down her soul still fight
for freedom and
thrive to be her own knight
she knows the night maybe so long
but in the end
she will find the place
where she will be belong
she will spread her wings
and take the flight
and will fly among the cloud so bright

Nandita Nandan

this time no storm can steal her dreams
and leave her
with a question "why"
she will fight it like
she owns the whole sky
so let her spread her wings
and fly
and touch the star before she dies
she was made to fly since beginning
and this time nothing can clip her wings.

Invisible strings

He kissed me like a man drowning
in the weight of sins not yet written
as if his lips could beg for forgiveness
even while his hands had the chance
to betray and pull me closer to ruins
it wasn't something simple as kiss
I can't even tell what it was as
I am too consumed to tell
where his need ended and mine began
And in that moment, I wondered
if he was trying to burn me alive
so that he could be the one
to put out the fire
the force of it wasn't love, not entirely
it was something sharper
hard enough to tattoo itself into my bones
soft enough to make me question
if the lust had ever existed
in this world so deep i wondered
if I would ever belong to myself again
whatever it was, it wasn't meant to soothe
It wasn't meant to be kind
And maybe that's why it consumed me
because it refused to fit inside the walls
of what I thought love could be
And then, as if recoiling from the violence
of his own hunger, he reached out
his hand trembled
brushing against my lips like

Nandita Nandan

a man erasing blood
from a crime he couldn't undo
but it wasn't tenderness
No, tenderness has limits
each stroke of his fingers rewrote the destruction
not to erase it, but to remake it
to shape the ruin into something
he could hold without guilt
but it hurt God, it hurt because
that gentleness demanded a vulnerability
that the kiss itself, never dared to ask for
that cut deeper than any bruise he could have left
It reached places inside me
I hadn't known were vulnerable
places I hadn't known could ache
It wasn't the kiss I carried with me
It was the wiping after
It was the way he tried to erase himself from me
and in doing so
left even more of himself behind
that touch didn't heal
It unearthed something buried
something ancient and raw
a wound I didn't remember receiving
but had always felt.
And in that moment
I didn't know what broke me more

Invisible strings

the possibility
that I might love him less by the end,
or the unbearable truth
that by breaking me in ways
only he could,
he was trying to love me more.

Nandita Nandan

His heart leaped with anticipation
at the sight of her typing indication
he waited for her message
with bated breath
hoping it would bring him happiness
but then he tried to type a reply
and a gallery reminder caught his eye
It was just a screenshot
nothing more
his heart sank
as he felt unsure
he realized that he had been mistaken
his happiness was just a dream
that he had taken
he had let his heart get carried away
and now he was left
with nothing to say.
but then he remembered
it's not about the end
it's about the journey

Invisible strings

the message that he meant to send
He smiled, and he started to type
Hoping that his words
would bring some light
And even though
it wasn't what he thought
He knew that his message
was still worth a shot
He hit send, and he waited for a reply
Hoping that it would bring a smile
to her eye.

Nandita Nandan

I stand before the mirror
naked and bare
my skin marred with scars
my lips chapped and fair
my eyes are blurred, I cannot see
the beauty that others claim
is within me
I trace my fingers along the scars and cuts
Each one a reminder
of my pain and my guts
I tell myself they're pretty
that they make me unique
but deep down I know
it's just an excuse I seek
I'm not naked, I'm decorated
In crimson red scars and cuts
I'm elevated
I wear them proudly for all to see
a symbol of my strength
of my bravery
for though the world may judge me
land call me weak
but I know that I'm strong
that I'm not meek.

Invisible strings

I've battled demons, and come out alive
And for that, I'll wear my scars with pride
So I stand before the mirror
naked and bare
And though I may not see
I know that I'm rare
For I'm a warrior, a fighter, a survivor
And my scars are just proof
of my inner fire.

Nandita Nandan

Untill I grace the graveyard

The shattered remains of past
Reminds me of a reality
that couldn't last
Of dreams faded into past
Now just a memory forged
into my heart
Which will remain with me
until I become remains of graveyard

A stomach in chaos -

A fluttering creature, delicate and light
A butterfly lost
in my stomach takes flight
Its wings beat softly
a symphony of grace
As it dances within, leaving a trace
Its colors are vibrant
a kaleidoscope of hues
A sight to behold, a wonder to muse
It flits and it flutters
a dance of its own
A beauty so rare, a sight to be shown
So let the butterfly dance
let it soar
Let it take flight, forevermore
For in its beauty
I find my own
A reflection of love, a beauty unknown
Its wings beat with a gentle grace
A dance of beauty in this sacred space
that's the moment you know
you can even fall alone..
~ fall for yourself first

Nandita Nandan

A vision of beauty
that catches the eye
she comes out of rain
like a watercolor from sky
Her hair is damp and
her clothes are wet
But she looks like a painting
we'll never forget
The drops on her face
like diamonds they shine
And I can't help but think
she's a work of divine
Her eyes are like oceans
so deep and so blue
And I'm lost in them
like sailors in a stormy view
She walks with grace
like a dancer in the rain
And I'm mesmerized
like a moth to a flame
Her voice is like music
And I'm enchanted
like she is some magic

Invisible strings

She moves with grace
and her steps are light
as if she's dancing to a song
in the rainy night
her eyes are the color
of stormy gray skies
and her lips are the hue
of a rose in disguise
a masterpiece of nature
a sight for the eye
the colors around her
seem to come alive
as if they're painting a picture
that will survive
the greens are greener
the blues are bluer
and the world so cruel
just seems to be a rumour
and as she walks away
we're left in awe
of the beauty
that we just saw.

Nandita Nandan

"Why do you find beauty in the storm?"

Because it's a canvas of chaos,
a masterpiece of destruction
and creation
that paints the sky
with the colors of life and death.

Invisible strings

At life's dawn
we stand like a canvas
a white slate
untouched by any artist
they play with stroke
and paints some scratches
we gather scars
like it's mute's language
each one a tragedy
it falls over us, with the pull of gravity
each scar a constellation in the making
Every broken bone a thread
in the tapestry of life's awakening
but what of the pain that we must endure
And the wounds
that we can't seem to cure?
Is there a beauty in the brokenness we see
or it's just a reflection
of our own misery?

Nandita Nandan

And what of the stars that shine so bright
Are they a beacon of hope
or just a trick of the light?
But as we look up at the stars above
We can't help but question
if it's all just a bluff
For in the darkness that surrounds us all
We can't help but feel so small
So maybe the answer is not in the scars we bear
Or the stars that light up the night so fair
But in the darkness that we can't escape
And the pain that we feel
with each breath we take
For in the end, we are but mere mortals
Living out our lives
in these fragile crystal
But as we reach the end of our mortal days
We're left to ponder life's cruel
and twisted ways
For every scar and broken bone we've known
Is a reminder of how we've grown
And as we take our final breath
We're left with nothing
but the bitter taste of death
For in the end, we are but dust and bone
and all of life's beauty,is just a fleeting loan

The Art of letting go

He was a flame that I thought I could
tame But perhaps his true destiny
was to ignite another's heart
Her fervent longing for him
burned with an intensity
While my passion flickered
a mere shadow of its former self
I held him close
but she held him in her dreams
And in those ethereal realms
their hearts beat as one
While mine struggled to keep pace
a feeble attempt
To hold onto a love
that was never truly mine
I believed he was mine
a treasure to cherish
But the shooting star
granted her wish
and he slipped away
Like sand through my fingers
he was never truly mine
A bittersweet realization
that left my heart aching
Now I watch from afar
as she holds him close

Nandita Nandan

Whispering words of love
that were once meant for me
And though my heart may weep
I know that he was meant for her
For sometimes
the universe grants wishes
that we cannot control
So I release him
like a bird from its cage
And watch
as he soars towards her
his true home
For sometimes
the greatest act of love
is letting go
And allowing someone else's dreams
to come to life.

Invisible strings

Our love had passion
like flame that burned bright
But it flickered out
like a star in the hazy night
more like our love was a rose
so tender and sweet
But it withered away
like a crushed rose lying on the street
We were a dream
soaring high in the sky
But we woke up to reality
like a bird that can't fly
we were almost a fairytale
a storybook romance
But the pages turned to dust
without giving a second chance.

Nandita Nandan

As shadows move in the pale moonlight
The music plays, a mournful tune
The dance of death, a haunting sight
As death takes hold
and life is going to end soon
The dancers twirl, their steps so light
As they move
through the darkness of the night
Their faces pale
their eyes so cold
As they dance with death so bold
The rhythm quickens
the pace so fast
As death takes over, and life is past
As they dance with death
and fade away
The dancers spin, their bodies sway
The dance of death, a solemn thing
As life is lost, and death takes wing
The music fades, the dancers gone
As death moves on, and life goes on.

Invisible strings

The night was young, and the music was loud
as I dance alone in the middle of the crowd
The music was a siren's call
A Haunting melody
that made my heart crawl
I danced to a song only few knew
And got lost to a eyes
that was someone else view
I tried to hide it, Keep it locked inside
Even though I know it will be her name
you lips would ever recite
even though this music will take
143 seconds to end
still I can't help but pretend
and get lost in your scent
The music played on
and I danced through the night
Lost in the rhythm, the beat, and the light
I can't help but wish
we will be beautiful enough
that poet will consider to write
For I danced alone, lost in a sea of faces
Lost in a love
that was never meant to take places
My heart ached for you
but you were nowhere to be found

Nandita Nandan

And as the music stopped
I was left standing on shaky ground.
But as the lights came up
and the night drew to a close
I realized that
I had been dancing all alone
But still
I held onto the hope
that one day
you would find the traces of girl
who lost herself
just to see you and her combined
And though I danced alone
lost in a sea of faces
I still knew it will be your name
I would scribble
in every empty pages.
~A girl who lost herself for ages

Invisible strings

She walks with a smile on her face
A girl who seems to have found her place
But deep inside, she feels a void
A place where happiness is destroyed
She loves the storms, the wind, and the rain
They match the turmoil
inside her brain
She's a different person in the light of day
And at night, she's someone else in every way
In the daytime, she waits for the night
When she can be free from her inner fight
But when the darkness comes
she can't escape
Her thoughts and fears
they start to take shape
She's a puzzle of different personalities
A complex maze of human realities
A girl who's happy with her life
But still feels the emptiness of strife
She longs for a peace that's hard to find
A place where she can leave her worries behind
But until that day
she'll keep on walking
Without the inner fear
that someone is watching.

Nandita Nandan

She is the moon
glowing in night's embrace
with stars in her eyes
love etched on her face
her heart a prism of colors unknown
In her arms, I find solace
a place to call my own
her touch, a symphony
gentle and true
she loves me truly
as only she can do.

Tales I read last summer

you better be my lover
like all those tales I read last summer
come with a happy ending please
so I can brag that in this field
Atleast I hold expertise
I wanna experience it all
either be kissing in backyard
or walking hand in hand in upcoming fall
distract me by wishing
on twinkling stars
while you make me lose count
of all my scars
write me qoutes and lovely songs
it doesn't matter if you mess up
rhyming scale along
respond to all those letters I wrote
if it's not much to ask
make sure to leave some funny random code
but before that
you need to get lost in my eyes
and whisper "she is the one" taking deep sigh
but alas it won't be much of surprise
as we are already past our first encounter
with no chance of love at first sight
but still I must hold onto the hope
of you falling later but harder

you must compensate
with cotton candy
and let's be perfect enough
for them to wonder
"when will they marry? "
so everything is planned out
like those tales I read last summer
so it's now it's your time
to convert our status
from friends to lover
and be my perfect bread
to my butter.

Invisible strings

Yearning for a love
like the shining moon
where "bye" is never uttered
it's always "see you soon"
I dream of a love beyond reach
I fear like the old couple next door
who've weathered the years
I wonder if my desires are too much to ask
to find a love like theirs
a love meant to last
maybe I just want someone
who will scribble my name
on every foggy window frame
I want someone
who won't promise me stars
but who will try to know why
I try to hide my scars
i just want someone who won't hesitate
to paint the sun in my skies
even when i will only see
those burry yellow lines with my teary eyes
I want someone who won't
make me hide behind my bangs and black mask
to erase the fact I cried
for the understanding
for someone who'll try
to know the reasons
why my teary eyes were never dry.

Nandita Nandan

In the land of whimsy and wild delight
Where imagination takes flight
A random topic to explore
In poetic words, I shall adore
Let's venture into the world of socks
Those mismatched wonders, in various flocks
From polka dots to stripes so bold
They keep our feet from the cold
Or perhaps, a ponder on rubber duck
Floating in bathtubs, bringing luck
Their vibrant hues and squeaky quacks
Bring joy to children and adults' tracks
But wait, let's shift to cardboard boxes
Filled with mysteries and hidden foxes
From makeshift forts to spaceships high
They transport us to dreams in the sky
Oh, let's not forget the enchanting dance
Of raindrops on windows, a poetic trance
They tap and patter, a rhythmic beat
Creating melodies so sweet
And what about the humble paperclip
its versatility withholds no grip
Holding papers together with grace
A small hero, in the office space

Invisible strings

Now, let's delve into the world of keys
Unlocking doors with secret ease
The key to a heart, the key to a dream
Each holding a story, it may seem
Random topics, endless and vast
A playground for creativity, to be cast
In the realm of randomness
we find Poetic treasures
unique and kind.

Bleeding through my eyes, a pain so deep
My heart aches, it cannot sleep
The tears they fall, a steady stream
A nightmare that feels
like a gentle dream
And yet my lips, they lay in a smile
A facade that I, have kept for a while
I pretend that I'm okay and that I'm fine
But the pain inside, it's always mine
I bleed through my eyes, but no one sees
like it's hidden behind eclipse
so I let my tears
freeze a smile on my lips
I wish that I could scream and shout
But my lips, they stay sealed
without a doubt
For I fear that if I let it out
The pain will only grow and sprout
So I keep it in, I hold it tight
And pray that one day, I'll see the light
But until then, I'll bleed through my eyes
And keep my lips engraved

Invisible strings

In a smile my eyes may stop bleeding
as time flies
but still these frozen smiles
will be used
whenever I feel like crying.

Nandita Nandan

As the ice cream drips down her hand,
memories of a carefree childhood
slip away like sand
The night sky was an abyss of darkness,
with only the twinkling stars above
to provide any semblance of light
she stood outside
her eyes fixated
on the celestial bodies above
hoping to catch a glimpse
of a falling star
Her heart was heavy with the weight
of unfulfilled desires
and she longed for a glimmer
of hope to break through the darkness
that surrounded her
As she closed her eyes
she felt a sense of desperation
wash over her
She made a wish with all her might
hoping that the universe
would hear her plea

Invisible strings

But as she opened her eyes
the stars remained still,
unresponsive to her yearning
The silence was deafening
and felt a sense of despair
creeping up on her
She couldn't help but feel
a sense of isolation
as if the universe
was conspiring against her
The darkness that enveloped her
was suffocating, and she felt
as if she was drowning
in a sea of sadness
Her heart ached
with the weight of
unfulfilled dreams
and she couldn't help but wonder
if she was destined to live a life
of unfulfilled desires

Nandita Nandan

As she stood there
gazing up at the sky
she couldn't help
but feel a sense of hopelessness
The stars that had once
brought her comfort
now seemed like a cruel reminder
of all that she had lost
The night was a canvas of sadness
and she was a mere speck
in the vast expanse of the universe
she saw a crumbled paper boat
floating in a nearby puddle
It reminded her of her childhood
of the times
she used to make paper boats
with her parents and
sail them in the rain
But now, her parents were gone
and she was all alone
she picked up the paper boat
and held it close to her heart.

Invisible strings

She felt a crushing pain inside
as if her heart was being squeezed
by a giant hand
She missed her parents so much
and she wished
they were still here with her
She walked back inside
and as she passed by a vase of roses
she noticed one of them was crushed
it reminded her of her own life
of how it had been crushed
and destroyed by the tragic accident
that took away her parents.
she sat down on the couch
feeling lost and alone
She wondered why life
had to be so cruel
why she had to suffer so much
She missed her childhood
the carefree days
when she could play and
laugh without a care in the world

Nandita Nandan

But now, she was forced to
grow up too fast
to take care of herself and
fend for herself
She missed out on so much,
and she knew she could never
get those moments back
As she closed her eyes
and let out a deep sigh
she realized that her childhood
was gone forever
And she knew that
she would never be the same again.

Invisible strings

In the gentle murmur
did I dance through a love saga
choreographed by fate's cruelest time?
Every step, drawing me closer
to someone who could only be touched
in the spaces of poetic rhyme
Beneath the stars soft glow
I patiently stay
and you kissed another lips,
whispering "star," as I fade away
No change in me
though I try to be more you
As I still remain someone
you never knew.
In their constant inquiries
they inquire about the one
behind each of my poetic line
and I can't help but lie
about you being a fiction
I weaved over a drunken sip of wine

Nandita Nandan

In the silence of the night's embrace
I chose defiance
left without a trace
With blade in hand and bloodied rhyme
I reclaimed my voice, a poet's prime
Through cuts and tears, my soul did bleed
Each verse a testament, a sacred creed
But your cold indifference, a bitter sting
Left me adrift on sorrow's wing
Now as I lie, skin turned pale
Your absence paints, a haunting tale
For in the depths of your cold blue hue,
My crimson whispers fade from view
You never touched, never dared
To trace the lines my soul bared
Soiled gray by your neglect's decay
I wonder if letting you choke
was the better way
But You never dared to touch, to feel
My heart's raw ache, too dark to heal
So I chose the blade,
the final spree,
"I slit my throat before you could choke me."

Invisible strings

Now I search for constellation
in the scars on my wrist
fingertips caressing them
like they are the only places
where your lips
have ever kissed.

Nandita Nandan

In the stillness of the night
she lies awake
tangled in sheets
longing for a connection deep
or just a moment of heat
as his fingers played with her raven hair
she wonders if his touch is sincere
or just a playful affair
she gave herself away
to mend his fractured soul
but why she feels regret rising her chest?
when atleast one of them is now whole
He saw her without clothes
but why she never felt naked under his gaze?
and whenever he said he knew her
somehow it felt just like a phrase.

Invisible strings

Beneath the quilt of night
where stars softly gleam
I'd snatch them for you
turning dreams into my poetic scheme
But, in this cosmic act
a question rings true,
Will you blame the thief
or admire the stolen view?
your stares looks beautiful on me
In the ocean of gazes
It's your eyes, that sets me free
You confessed likings
for my playlist's embrace
Little did you know, in every beat
it's your trace
How to reveal that in every lyrical hue
Resides the echo of my love, painted in you?
you often ask me why do I write
so listen
who would defend my love for you
if not poetries
in this hazy night.

Nandita Nandan

In the realm of dreams
where romantic plays hold sway
She dream of tales in the light of day
Of unicorns prancing in meadows serene
But shadows lurk, unseen and keen
Beneath the stars, a twisted ballet
She dream of whispers that lead astray
Fairies laugh in a moonlit trance
Yet nightmares breed
in the innocent dark dance
As the dream unfurls, innocence fray
she dream of endings in mysterious ways
A once-sweet lullaby turns to a scream
In the her every dreams
murder takes the scene.

Invisible strings

Beneath the fabric of smiles she wears
A hidden atlas of wounds
life declares
Scars etched like whispers
a map untold
Leading to places where stories unfold
Her laughter, a portrait
painted with care
A masterpiece of disguise
she has learned to wear
Look into the depths
past the veiled guise
In the reflection of her eyes
truth lies.

Nandita Nandan

A cascade of tears
a silent ballet
In hidden corners
where shadows play
Tracks on her face
from eyes to her chin,
Echoes of years,
letting sorrows win.

Invisible strings

what if you are watching me
whenever I look away?
can I assume
you visit that place
because I am always in that café
is there still a chance
of you dreaming about me every day?
what if you chose to admire me from far
just because I was looking away..

Nandita Nandan

I lay here in my bed,
with tears streaming down my face
As my husband takes what's his
with no regard for my disgrace
He thinks he has the right
to take from me what he wants
But I'm a person too,
with feelings and with thoughts
The society thinks it's okay
that a husband can do what he pleases
But I know that it's not right
that my body's not his to seize
I've tried to tell them all
that I'm not just a possession
But they don't want to listen
As they don't want, to be questioned
I dream of a world
where women are treated with respect
Where their bodies are their own
and their voices are not checked
But for now, I'm trapped here
in this prison of my own
With a husband who thinks it's okay
to take what he's already known

Invisible strings

So if you see me on the street
with bruises on my skin
Don't judge me for my choices
or the pain that I am in
I'm a person too, with feelings
and with thoughts
And I deserve to be treated
with the respect that I've been taught.

Nandita Nandan

On my pinky finger
promises secure
once love adorned
a vow so pure
yet now you wield
your middle finger's sting
swearing in anger
our bond unwinding
from innocence to resentment
we linger
A gesture once tender
now a painful trigger
how the world has shifted
yet we still linger
from my pinky finger
to your middle finger.

Invisible strings

She fell first, and harder too
her heart was open
fresh and new
and though she tried to hide her love
It shone through
like a beacon above
she fell for him, with all her heart
and knew that
they were worlds apart
but still she loved, with all her might
And dreamed of him
both day and night
she fell first, and harder too
and though he loved her this much
he knew he couldn't give her all
she sought and so he hesitated
he fought
he loved her too, with all his heart
But couldn't bear to see her fall apart
And so he held back
and watched as she struggled
bit by bit
but still she loved with all her soul
and dreamed of him
to make her whole

Nandita Nandan

And though he couldn't give her all
She loved him still
through rise and fall
For love is like a river
wild and free
And though it flows, it's never easy
But still she loved
with all her heart
And knew that they would never part.
For though she fell first, and harder too
Her love was strong
pureand true
And though he hesitated,he fought
But He loved her too
with all he has got.

That same old cardigan

In the corner of my mind
There's a memory I can't leave behind
A cardigan draped over a chair
A symbol of a love that was once there
I slip it on and feel the chill
Of a love that once gave me a thrill
I wear it now, to feel your touch
To remember the love
that meant so much
But now you're gone and I'm all alone
Left with nothing
but this cardigan to hold
But now it's just a faded dream
A reminder of what
could have been

Nandita Nandan

I lie here, counting heartbeats
each one stammering your name
like a prayer
it's too afraid to finish
Tell me, my love
how can a thought
weigh more than a body
how can you feel more closer
than my own skin?
If sleep ever comes
it will not find me whole
I've scattered myself
across the night
in fragments
only you could understand
Yet here you are,
the one dream I can never have
and the only reason
I'll never wake.
I tell myself to forget
to rest
but how does one forget a fire
when their veins are rivers of gasoline?

Invisible strings

a storm that feels like home
a whisper louder
than any scream
So tonight, I let you consume me
Let the stars watch
and the night keep count
of how many times, your name
has replaced my heartbeat
how longing can feel like suffocation
but taste like honey
If sleep comes, it will not find me
How can it
when my soul refuses to rest
until it has memorized
the way your laugh folds the air
the way your presence
feels like gravity
rewriting the laws of existence.

Nandita Nandan

And then somedays
she went nameless too...